Before You Pack Your Bag

PREPARE YOUR HEART

Short-Term Mission Preparation Guide
with 12 Bible Studies
plus Trip Journal

CINDY JUDGE

About the author

Cindy Judge is committed to inspiring those going on short-term missions to Christ-honoring teamwork and servanthood in a new culture. Having traveled on three continents with youth, adults, and her family, she knows the value of preparation. Being a missions graduate of Moody Bible Institute, associate campus director with Campus Crusade for Christ, trainer of 25 teams a year at Willow Creek Community Church for 10 years and presently on the Cross-cultural Ministry staff at Wheaton Bible Church, Cindy writes with a passion to create solid training materials integrated with God's Word.

Before You Pack Your Bag Prepare Your Heart by Cindy Judge
©2000 by Campfire Resources, Inc. All rights reserved.

Design by Sue Lundin

Before You Pack Your Bag Prepare Your Heart is produced and published by Campfire Resources, Inc., Wheaton IL; and distributed by STEM*Press*, Minneapolis MN.

Campfire **Resources**
Connecting Leaders to Answers and Each Other.

To order more copies:
- download an order form at www.campfireresources.com,
- fax it to (952)996-1384, or
- mail it to STEM*Press*, PO Box 386001, Minneapolis MN 55438. Or
- order online at www.STEMmin.org, or
- call (952)996-1385 (toll-free 1-877-783-6646).

Table of Contents

108358

Introduction

People go on short-term mission trips for many reasons. Having trained hundreds of short-term mission team members, I have heard all sorts of reasons:

- to have an adventure
- to serve the poor
- to tell lost people about Jesus
- to build a house
- to be an encouragement
- to spend time with a friend

During an orientation session, I asked the members of one group why they wanted to go on the mission trip. One guy boldly blurted out his reason, "Well, I just got dumped by my girlfriend, and I have to get out of the country."

You have your own personal reasons. God also has His reasons for wanting you on this trip, some of which you already know and some you can hardly guess. I have a core conviction that short-term mission trips are life changing for you *and* for those you go to serve. However, I believe that positive life-change occurs in direct proportion to how prepared you are. No doubt you have a lot to do before you go, but a prepared heart should be the number one priority on your list.

In the remaining weeks before the trip, pick up your Bible, and use this preparation guide. You will find 12 different insights. Some lessons will help you walk into diverse surroundings with less fear and more sensitivity. You will be challenged to learn to tell your story, be a strong team member, and be a good guest. But most of all, the Holy Spirit will begin to strengthen you and build into you qualities that reflect Jesus to those you serve. Ask God to use this guide to prepare your heart *before* you pack your bag.

Lesson one

"Whatever it takes!"

When a person responds to a request with, "OK, whatever it takes," it suggests a willing attitude and desire to do the job.

Short-term mission projects are all about "whatever it takes." From singing on street corners to painting walls to playing soccer to pulling teeth, short-termers find ways to bring God's love to people.

Crossing cultural barriers and reaching out to advance the cause of Jesus Christ is no small thing. Missionaries have been motivated by the spirit of "whatever it takes" throughout all history. Through your experience, you will begin to understand this motivation that permeates the world of missionary service.

The Bible study preparation of this book will help you define what it will take from you to advance the cause of Christ through your trip. As you understand the goals of your project and step up to the challenge of your role, pray that God will give you an attitude of "whatever it takes" to obey His directions and give honor to Him.

Begin by looking at the foundational truths from the New Testament book of Matthew. Jesus taught His followers some very significant truths about His perspective on our service.

In Matthew 25:31-46, Jesus tells his disciples that He will sit on His throne someday with the nations gathered before Him. He explains to us how He looks at the service we do. Read the passage and write out at least five things we can do for those in need.

What are we reminded of in verse 40?

A few chapters later, Jesus is meeting with His followers for the last time on earth. In Matthew 28:18-20, we read the final instruction Jesus gave to all His followers. As you read Jesus' words, write out the specific things that we are told to do.

What is the truth in verse 18 that is essential to your ability to do "whatever it takes" to share God's love?

What does this mean for you?

Think about these two Matthew passages in relationship to your particular mission project. Write out some ways you will follow these directions.

Lesson two

What's in this for you? What's in this for them?

It's amazing how many people benefit from a short-term mission trip. One church group came up with 37 distinct benefits of sending a mission team. These benefits will flow in three different directions: toward those you serve, your group, and yourself.

Some benefits to those you serve:
- You bring fresh energy, willing hands, and encouragement to your hosts, both the missionary and the national.
- You provide the resources or know-how to fulfill a need.
- Your host experiences community with the larger body of Christ as you worship and work together.
- Some may come to Christ.

Some benefits to your group:
- What you learn in another culture shapes and brings new perspectives into the group.
- Leadership abilities grow and become stronger.
- Others are encouraged to grow by stepping out of their comfort zones through observing the group in action.
- People live out newly examined values in light of a larger worldview when they return to their home church.
- The group gains a new vision and enthusiasm for serving at home.

Some personal benefits:
- Make new friends with your team and hosts.
- Be challenged to grow spiritually.
- Use your gifts to build the body of Christ.
- Grow a larger heart for the lost and needy.
- Learn to live and love in the diversity of another culture.
- Experience fulfillment as you strive to learn, love, and serve in the name of Jesus.

That's a pretty impressive list, isn't it? Yet when you return home from your trip, you will add some benefits of your own.

Looking at these lists can also be a little intimidating. Can God do all this through you and in you? You're likely to experience dependence on Him in a whole new way. You will need to depend on His power, not your own.

Take a pen, and put a check mark beside the benefits on the previous page that you get most excited about. Pray for these things to become a reality.

In the book of Ephesians, we find some real encouragement about depending on God. In Ephesians 3:14-21, we see what God's power can do. Record three ways that His power can help you.

1.

2.

3.

Now take some time to write out a prayer about your need to depend on God's power and not your own in light of your responsibilities on your mission trip.

Lesson three

"How" is more important than "what"

Many mission projects are about providing some kind of construction work, like building a house. Some projects involve ministry at a church, like a Vacation Bible School. It's easy to look at the kind of activity you do as an end in itself. Moving a family from a house of cardboard to a new cinderblock home or teaching about Jesus are worthy goals and important accomplishments in the name of God.

But let's look deeper than the "what" of a project and explore the "how." We know that God cares deeply about our attitudes. It's about more than just doing something worthwhile. It's about serving: serving with a right attitude, one that exemplifies Christ.

Jesus was on a mission when He left His home in heaven and came to earth. He had much to accomplish. He healed the sick, helped men catch fish for their livelihood, and taught the lost that He was their Savior. But let's also look at *how* He did these things.

Read Philippians 2:1-8. Then write out the instructions Paul gives us in verses 3-5.

Looking at verses 6-8, trace the steps Jesus took as He left heaven, came to earth, and eventually died for us. Write out the steps He took. Next to each step, write how He did it.

<u>What He did</u>   <u>How He did it</u>

Having an attitude of humility is easier said than done. We, as North Americans, are not known for our humility. North Americans often have more of an attitude of selfishness and even superiority. To look out for and serve others before ourselves is very difficult. It is the opposite of what we are taught by our peers. Being a humble servant does not come naturally.

Whatever the tasks of your mission project, whether digging a ditch, taking care of the sick, or doing mundane chores, your attitude will mean the most. God wants to build the qualities of a humble servant into your character.

Jesus spoke about an attitude of superiority in Mark 10:42-45. What do those who act superior do? What is the great paradox of servanthood?

Considering the environment and the work you will do on your trip, what are some practical ways you can be a humble servant and avoid acting superior?

Read the promises of Philippians 1:6 and 2:13. Write out the phrases that give you confidence that you can have a Christlike attitude.

Lesson four

Traveling outside your comfort zone

It's a good bet you'll pack your favorite remedies for common ailments on the trip. There's that pink lotion for bug bites and the other pink medicine for when you're "intestinally challenged." But what are you packing for culture shock? Have you heard of that ailment?

What is culture shock anyway? To help understand it, let's imagine this scenario: When you arrive at your site, the warm weather feels so lovely, the little village seems quaint and friendly, and your hosts are so interested and neighborly. But . . . after a few weeks or maybe even days, you feel your attitudes shift. The honeymoon is definitely over. Suddenly the heat is stifling, the tiny village is closing in on you, and your hosts won't give you a moment to yourself. Is that culture shock? Let's start with a definition.

Culture shock is the disorientation that results from unfamiliar surroundings and unmet expectations.

Culture shock has begun. Nothing is predictable, and daily living is filled with an uncomfortable feeling. Now you find yourself critical and complaining . . . and disappointed for even feeling this way. You may even feel like going home.

Just remember that these are all very normal feelings for anyone who travels outside his or her own culture. So even though you may expect to experience some degree of culture shock, let's look at it carefully and see if it can be a bit less electrifying.

What happens when living outside of one's own culture? After the initial honeymoon stage, one of the first things to creep in is a judgmental attitude. If things are different from one's own customs, values, and behaviors, they are, well . . . just wrong or intolerable, or at the least, just plain weird.

Think about this. It's even true when you get close to another person or family here at home. When they do something differently than you do, it's common to think that **you** do **it** the right way and they do **it** the wrong way.

Think of an example from your own experience of another person or family doing "it" wrong, and write it out.

In every culture we can find unbiblical practices. But experts say that people from every culture around the world think their way is the right way. This is called ethnocentricity. It is very important to learn early that the social behaviors of another culture are not necessarily wrong; they are just different from yours. They can be appreciated and enjoyed. Try to memorize this phrase, and remind yourself of it often. **"IT'S NOT WRONG; IT'S JUST DIFFERENT."**

The famous short-term missionary Paul lived in and out of many different cultures. Read in I Corinthians 10 about Paul's dealing with an agitated group who thought eating certain meat was wrong. In verses 23-33, he addresses this issue. Write out two principles that you want to remember from verses 31-33.

1.

2.

Lesson five

Are you an American first or a Christian first?

How can you really get to know the people you're going to serve? It can take years to really understand people from a different culture. You know you won't be there for very long. Let's press the pause button and consider this approach first. The experts tell us that understanding other cultures can begin with having an understanding of our own culture.

First we have a few words that represent some positive stereotypes or traits of North Americans.
- *friendly* • *outgoing* • *hardworking* • *generous*
- *well-educated* • *reliable* • *confident*

Sounds great. Makes you proud to be an American! In fact some of these qualities may be among your personal motives for wanting to go on a mission project in the first place. These qualities may have their roots in your cultural heritage.

Take a moment today to ask someone to describe an American. What terms did he or she come up with?

There are other not-so-positive stereotypes attached to North Americans:
- *materialistic* • *wasteful* • *domineering*
- *arrogant* • *disrespectful of authority* • *corrupt*

These more negative traits come from the darker side of our culture. They come from sinful patterns through the years. This may be an important time to look a bit deeper within yourself. Is your life influenced by some of these negative traits? Ask yourself a probing question, are you an American first or a Christian first?

Much of the success of fitting in and serving those in another culture will be related to how we deal with these negative stereotypes. As we accept and grapple with these harmful traits, as Christians, there is good news . . . we do have the power not to be controlled by them through Christ.

We know that God is in the business of transforming our lives as we give ourselves to Him. In Romans 12:2, Paul pleads with Christians not to be conformed to this world, but to be transformed by the renewing of our minds. Therefore, let's get some help from a powerful passage in Phillipians.

Read Philippians 3:7-21. If we desire to become everything God wants us to be, what encouragement do we find in verses 12-16?

We read in verses 18 and 19 that some have their minds saturated with the attitudes and values of today's culture. Yet verses 20 and 21 remind us that as Christians, our citizenship is in heaven. What does that mean to you personally?

Lesson six

Learn their story; tell yours

Some people are great storytellers by nature. Others have to work at it. But one thing is for sure, people love to hear a story. Telling stories is a way of life in many cultures. When you show interest in the story of someone you meet from another culture, you may win a new friend. Find an interpreter, if you need one, and listen to people's stories. Then be ready to tell your own.

When you visit other cultures, people are curious and will want to know why you have come. How will you answer this? "To work on a building" or "to teach a class" may be appropriate answers, but perhaps there is a better answer. Maybe this is an opportunity to articulate more than the obvious. Maybe this is an open door to share the spiritual dimension of your answer. Sometimes telling your story may include how Christ has motivated you to serve.

Another situation that may occur as you visit a church is that the pastor may ask you to "give a greeting." Your group might be tempted to stand up, wave and nod, and then sit back down. However, in most places, this request is for far more than that kind of greeting. It means that someone from your group will be expected to go up front and speak. How are you going to respond to this opportunity? The best response would be to count it the perfect time to not only bring a greeting from your country, but have someone share his/her story or testimony.

Read I Peter 3:15, and write out the encouragement from Paul.

In I Timothy 4:12-16 Paul challenges his young disciple, Timothy.
In what ways was he supposed to be an example?

Take some time over the next few weeks to work on your story. It may be about how you first came to Christ or possibly some later event in your journey of faith. It is always good to think of your audience. As you begin to work on your story, think of the things you have in common with those you are going to serve. There are many universal aspects to life like family, school, work, marriage, etc. There are also the universal themes of life like the pursuit of happiness, peace of mind, individual dignity, security, etc. There are negative themes that plague all of us, like the host of sins that we deal with or feelings like fear, anger, or disappointment. These matters touch everyone... regardless of your place on the planet.

So, as you reflect upon your life, you will want to ask the Lord for wisdom and help you as you write your unique, yet universal story.

Some questions to answer as you work on your story:

- How did I realize my need for a Savior **or** how did Jesus meet me in my time of need?

- How can I clearly explain how to accept God's love and forgiveness through my story?

- What difference have I experienced in my life because of accepting God's love and forgiveness?

- What are some specific attitudes, actions and motivations that have changed?

Practice your story and ask for feedback. Keep it simple, don't use exclusively Christian or popular jargon that won't translate, and practice speaking in short phrases as you may be giving your story through an interpreter.

Lesson seven

So what are you so afraid of?

Facing a group of middle-aged women, I informed them of a new twist in the plans for their first mission trip. We were going to be staying in the homes of nationals from the church we were serving in the barrio . . . instead of a downtown hotel. I saw a wave of panic wash over their usually enthusiastic faces. New fears had been born in an instant. Fears of eating weird foods, of sleeping who knows where, of scary bathroom facilities. Things had taken a sharp turn off the highway and onto an unknown, curvy road.

There are all sorts of fears that sneak up on us when we're preparing to serve in another country. It is a good idea to acknowledge some of these fears before the trip. Some are more severe than others, but they can be paralyzing.

One person may fear whether the plane will land on time. Another will be worried about whether the plane will land at all. There are bugs and things that go bump in the night and there may be little things that are secret fears, like getting homesick or having a bad hair week. We all have them. Let's start with identifying some of your fears.

Jot down a few of your own fears, including your secret ones.

Remember that many fears will dissipate as you learn about your geographical setting, ask questions of your hosts, and begin to understand the circumstances that can induce those fears. Remember that your hosts may be having some fears of their own regarding you. After all, you are a stranger to them too. So the first step may be to ask good questions to get to know each other and allay some of your fears that way. However, you may still be burdened with some fears.

One of the most common sayings of Jesus found frequently throughout the Gospels is "Fear not." You may be asking yourself how it is possible to not feel fear about the things that will confront you on the trip.

In Luke 12:22-31, Jesus reasons with His disciples about the things that concern them. Read this passage, and summarize in your own words the concerns mentioned in verses 22-23.

Write down what Jesus teaches about common worries.
   From verses 24-26

   From verses 27-31

The passage in Luke gives us God's perspective on some physical worries and fears. There are other kinds of fears as well. In Philippians 4:6-7, Paul gives us another means to finding God's peace over our fears. What are we encouraged to do?

Lesson eight

Which is better, a vacuum cleaner or a broom?

"Heads up!" is an expression of warning commonly used when someone is about to get clunked by a flying object. Well, here is a "heads up" about a common cross-cultural issue that often clunks short-termers and makes them fall.

Most Americans are great workers and put a high priority or value on doing a task with utmost efficiency. Remember the "hard-working" stereotype? There is an old adage that one doesn't play until the work is done. Most Americans actually enjoy getting a job done . . . and the faster, the better!

Let's look at an example from our culture: the floor is dirty. The smartest, easiest, and most efficient method of cleaning the floor has been invented—the vacuum cleaner. Every year there are newer and better vacuum cleaners on the market. The new ones are lighter, have more suction, and now have directional lights . . . all to clean your carpets easier, faster, and more efficiently. This is important to us. Investing in a product to do the job quicker and better than the old method is a no-brainer.

Now let's consider the people in the country where your team is going. Possibly for thousands of years, the floors have been cleaned in the same way: with a broom. No one's complaining. No one seems to be looking for a better method. Would anyone in these countries want the vacuum cleaner that was just described? Probably not.

The broom-users are happy to sweep and may choose to spend time talking with a friend who just dropped by while they are sweeping. Efficiency may never have crossed their minds.

Many cultures value their relationships higher than anything else and put little value in doing a task most efficiently.

Now here is the "heads up". If we are to be servants with the humility and love of Christ, we need to show openness and acceptance to the way of life of our hosts. When it comes to doing a task, you may be tempted to think and act more like an American than a Christian. When you're tempted to ask the typical American question, "How can this job be done better or faster?", you need to stop and remind yourself that this culture is operating with different values and that your question might be inappropriate or even disrespectful.

Demonstrating your acceptance of the way things are done in other countries shows honor, respect, and the love of Christ.

So remember:
- Be open to learning why they do things the way they do.
- It may not be important to introduce them to your favorite higher technology.
- You are trying to build relationships that honor the Lord, whom you represent.
- You have come to serve in whatever capacity is needed.
- You have come to learn from your new friends.
- You have come to accept and love brothers and sisters in Christ who are different from you.

Reread Philippians 2:3-4. Paraphrase these verses to concur with the points listed above. You may find this passage helpful to memorize.

Lesson nine

Top ten ways to be a good guest

It's not always easy to be a good guest. When you were little, your mother may have given you a few tips when you went to visit someone. It's not natural to know what's expected of you. Here is a list of practical tips on being a guest in a cross-cultural situation. Though you may never fully understand why, it's a pretty sure bet that these ten social hints (in no particular order) are universally acceptable for acting with sensitivity and humility.

1 **Show respect for your host by using the proper greetings and titles, especially to the eldest in the group.**

2 **Ask your new acquaintances about their families.**
You can show them pictures of your family, but leave out the ones of your U.S. standard house or car.

3 **Be a good observer and listener, and ask polite questions.**
Try not to talk too much—usually not a problem when you don't know the language.

4 **Dress appropriately to show honor to the culture.**
Women should dress modestly and have their shoulders covered. Women shouldn't wear shorts or pants unless given permission by the host organization. Men need to ask about wearing shorts also.

5 **Act very discreetly with the opposite sex.**
Avoid public displays of affection. For singles, avoid being seen alone or talking alone with the opposite sex. You can pursue any new relationships that may interest you when you get home.

6 **Always show gratitude for your accommodations and food, whatever they may be.**
You are most likely receiving the best they have to offer. Don't boast about what Americans have.

7 **Never show your temper.**
Many cultures see a display of anger as the greatest of sins.

8 **Be sure you get permission to photograph someone.**
Don't offend your hosts by taking photos of what may be considered private space or what is considered a negative aspect of the country.

9 **Show empathy and appreciation, not pity, for the surroundings.**
This is your new friends' home. Show respect for it, and if there are beggars in the area, ask your host how to deal with them since local philosophies and practices vary from place to place.

10 **Be flexible with your time.**
Go with the flow of the culture and the ministry you're involved with. Go to learn and serve, not to keep track of the time. Remember what they say about Americans: "They have the watches, but we have the time."

Read Romans 15:1-9. Why should we seek to please others?

In verse 5, what is the worthy goal for being unified with brothers and sisters in Christ from another culture?

In reviewing the ten hints, circle the number of the ones that will be the most challenging for you to follow. Pray about each one. You may want to discuss the difficult points with your teammates.

Lesson ten

Being a team player

Anyone who has ever played on a sports team knows the importance of being a team player. Playing next to someone who knows the game and puts in 100% effort makes all the difference in how much you enjoy the game.

The importance of being a team player will become obvious as you begin your trip. Things like giving your best, following directions, and sharing the work load are important to any successful team effort—whether it's a sports team or a mission team. And remember that few of us have ever played on a team that we live and work with 24 hours a day.

So, how can you get "in shape" for a team like this? As in any team, developing as a team player requires equal parts of good coaching and right attitudes. Let's begin with some coaching from the apostle Paul. His analogy for teamwork in Romans 12 is the body of Christ.

Read the vision of Paul, the coach, in Romans 12:4-5. Each person will make a unique contribution to the team. How are our relationships to one another described?

Continue reading in verses 6-8. According to what you know about yourself right now, what are the gifts that you bring to this team?

In Romans 12:9-21 Paul coaches us with about 25 different commands for spiritual teamwork. Read them and write out at least ten that you want to remember and that challenge you the most.

1.

2.

3.

4.

5.

6.

7.

8.

9.

10.

It would be great if your team could "practice" as a team in some way before you actually arrive on foreign soil. Some teams make this a priority and work together on some project as a group before leaving home.

Most likely your team has a coach or team leader. He or she is responsible for the logistical concerns like tickets, schedules, and job assignments, as well as fostering a good atmosphere among the team members and managing unforeseen conflicts and difficult circumstances. Supporting your team leader's leadership is crucial to the success of your team. Think about how you can support and help your team leader.

Jot down some ideas for supporting the leader of your team.

Lesson eleven

What if a teammate drives you crazy?

The mission project is going great, the team is singing on the job, playing with the neighbor kids on breaks, and seeing people really open to the gospel message.

There is a common story that happens, though the details differ. Put fifteen Americans in another country, sweating over wheelbarrows full of concrete in 100° heat, eating rice and beans every day, sleeping on the concrete floor of a church . . . and someone is sure to get cranky.

Ask the cranky team member privately what is bothering him or her. Amazingly, the response may have nothing to do with the heat or the hardness of the floor. What's most likely to be driving him or her crazy is a fellow teammate with whom he or she works all day.

Why does this stuff happen? Shouldn't we all just get along? Or should we just expect these difficulties? It's important to remember that the enemy of our souls would like nothing more than to have us be defeated *within* the team. But you need to personally prepare for inevitable friction by looking at some steps for dealing with conflict . . . anywhere.

1. Take time to identify your feelings. What's going on inside you? Is it frustration, anger, fatigue? Before taking any action, pray about your feelings. Defeat the enemy by claiming God's control over the situation. A good night's sleep may help.
2. Define the cause. Are there external circumstances like the heat or the dirt causing aggravation? Or are there internal issues like a personality difference or a power struggle?
3. Take some steps. First pray about your side of the conflict. Decide how you are going to deal with the person with whom you have the conflict. Don't just stew about it.

Remember Jesus' story about the log and the speck in Matthew 7? Read the first five verses and write out the question to ask yourself in your own words.

From I Thessalonians 5:11-15, make a list of the attitude checks that you want to remind yourself of when facing a conflict with someone.

1.

2.

3.

4.

When you decide to confront someone:
- Find an appropriate time and place when both of you are calm and rested.
- Honor the ground rules of stating only your own issues.
- Honestly confront the issue.
- Ask forgiveness for your part.
- Seek restoration.
- Propose a compromise.
- Consider praying together.
- If you need another person's help, follow the pattern found in Matthew 18.

Lesson twelve

Track what happens on your trip

You will make memories for a lifetime. You can count on this trip marking your life in many ways. How can you track or record these experiences so you won't forget the impact when you get home? Let's explore three ways you can record and share your experience: taking pictures, keeping a journal, and telling about your experience after you return home.

1 For most Americans, one way to record and relive the moment comes through taking pictures. You will cherish the pictures you take on your trip forever. Your pictures will hold memories that will trigger precious times of learning and significant growth in your life.

However, a side note to remember is that it can be very disconcerting to your hosts to face flashing cameras throughout the days of your stay. It may feel like an invasion of privacy. Be sensitive. One tip to consider is assigning one photographer to take pictures on a particular day with the permission of the host. Then when you get home, get the reprints of the photos you desire.

Besides the memories of new friends and new experiences, God has much more in store for you. He will be working in and through you in new ways. Your influence on your host will remain. You will have learned much about the culture you lived in. It may mark a new beginning for you in the way you think or the direction your life will go in the future. You won't want to lose any extraordinary moments of learning and insight.

2 Keeping a journal is an effective way to capture the experiences. Record your feelings about your daily encounters: the stories about friendships with nationals, the way God intervenes in your day, what God is doing in your heart, new insights you learn about missions and doing God's work.

In the Bible we are encouraged to record and retell the things that God has done. The whole Bible is actually a compilation of the stories of God's people written by many authors who were God's inspired journal keepers.

The Psalms are filled with encouragement to remember all God has done. Read Psalm 78:1-7, and understand the far-reaching value of keeping a record of God's work. In Psalm 77:11-15, the writer is remembering all God has done. From verses 11-12, write out the verbs that tell us to focus on what God has done.

In verses 13-15, what are we reminded about God?

If this idea of keeping a journal is new to you, the following pages will provide you with some questions to help you get started when you're on your trip. Long after your trip, you will read your journal pages and reflect on what God did in and through you during your trip.

3 When you get back home, prepare to talk about your experience. Telling your stories to friends and family will be very important to you. Relate how God worked in your heart. Those close to you will want the long version. However, it is good to remind yourself that sometimes those who ask about your trip may just want a short review. You also may be called upon to speak at a church or group function. God may even open doors for you to share your faith with someone who has never heard. In every case take time to prepare your presentation.

God will honor the preparation you have done for your short-term mission trip. It will be exciting to record what you have learned. You will be grateful that you prepared your heart before you packed your bag.

Journal entry 1

In what ways was I stretched beyond my comfort zone today?

Journal entry 2

What surprised me the most today about this culture?
What are my feelings about this day?

Journal entry 3

**What strengths am I seeing in a fellow team member today?
Have I told him/her?**

Journal entry 4

What have I learned today from a person among our hosts?
What is God impressing upon me today?

Journal entry 5

What did I feel I contributed today? How did I use my gifts today?

Journal entry 6

Have I seen oppression here? Is it physical, spiritual, or of what nature? What effect does it have on me?

Journal entry 7

**What was one struggle I faced with someone today?
How did/should I handle it?**

Journal entry 8

What is God impressing upon my heart today?

Journal entry 9

How do I feel about being a part of God's plan for this time and place in these people's lives?

Journal entry 10

What are some things about my life at home that I want to examine in light of things I've learned here?

40

Notes

Notes

Notes

Notes

Notes

Notes

Recommended reading

The Essential Guide to the Short Term Mission Trip by David C. Forward, Moody Press, Chicago, Illinois.
Successful Mission Teams by Martha VanCise, New Hope Publishers, Birmingham, Alabama.
Mack and Leeann's Guide to Short-Term Missions by J. Mack and Leeann Stiles, InterVarsity Press, Downers Grove, Illinois.
MISTM-Maximum Impact Short-Term Mission by Roger Peterson, Gordon Aeschliman and R. Wayne Sneed, STEM Press, Minneapolis, MN.
Reentry Guide for Short-Term Mission Leaders by Lisa Espinelli Chinn, Deeper Roots Publications & Media, Orlando, FL
Foreign to Familiar, Sarah A. Lanier, McDougal Publishing, Hagerstown, MD.

How to use this study guide for your team

As a Team Leader or a host your role is much more than tending to the myriad of logistics to make the mission trip a reality. You have the potential of creating an opportunity for God to work in each team members' life by motivating each individual to spend time in God's word while doing these lessons.

If you are a short-term mission team leader:

One of the most important responsibilities you have is to help the team prepare spiritually. Start out by ensuring that each member has his or her own book. Encourage accountability by assigning the Bible study lessons on a specific schedule during the months before departure. To solidify the concepts, try these ideas:

- You may use lessons 2, 3, 4, 5, 6, 8, and 9 as the outline for your teaching during orientation sessions.
- After a teaching time, divide the group into smaller accountability groups of 3-4 people to discuss the content and what each person is learning.
- During the trip, review pertinent lessons especially chapters 3, 9, 10, and 11 as a way of troubleshooting issues.
- Use some of the Journal Entry questions during meal times or travel times on the trip in order to debrief together. This is a great opportunity for team members to open up and learn from one another.

If you are a team leader who will meet the team members for the first time on the ministry site:

It's hard to predict how much preparation team members will receive before you meet them. Send each team member a book 6-8 weeks before they arrive.

- Require that each team member complete the lessons prior to arrival and be prepared to discuss the lessons.
- During an orientation day, discuss lessons 3, 4, and 5.
- Use Lesson 9 on the second day and Lessons 8 and 10 on consecutive days for morning sharing times.

If you are hosting a mission team:

To help ensure that the team will arrive more spiritually preprared to serve, and have been introduced to concepts of cross-cultural sensitivity, use the book in this way:

- Introduce the team leader to this book by sending him a book months prior to the trip and help him to understand the value of personal preparation.
- Require that each team member has a book and personally completes the lessons before arrival.
- Use the topics during orientation as suggested above. Review and contextualize the truths to your specific circumstances during debriefing times together early in their stay with you.